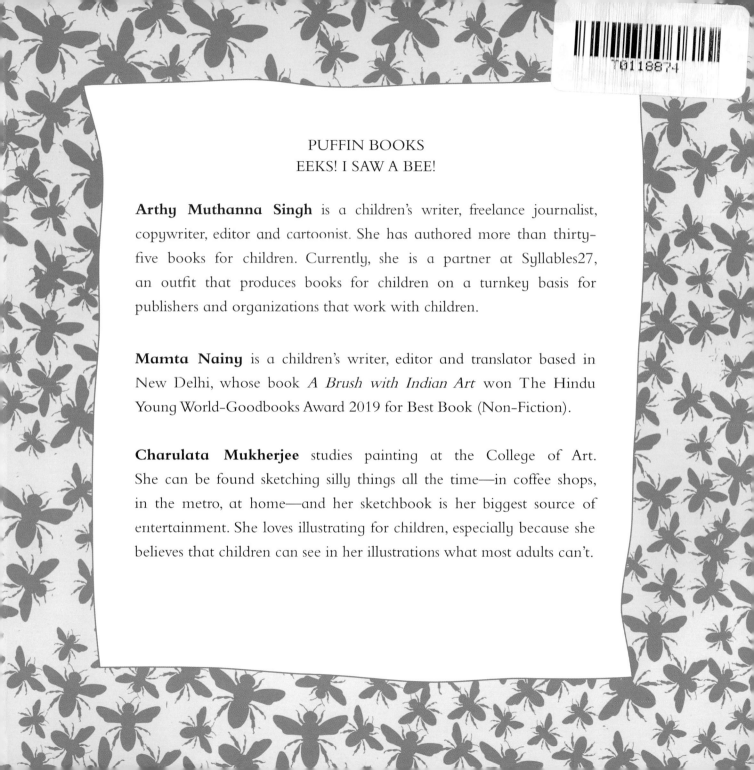

PUFFIN BOOKS
EEKS! I SAW A BEE!

Arthy Muthanna Singh is a children's writer, freelance journalist, copywriter, editor and cartoonist. She has authored more than thirty-five books for children. Currently, she is a partner at Syllables27, an outfit that produces books for children on a turnkey basis for publishers and organizations that work with children.

Mamta Nainy is a children's writer, editor and translator based in New Delhi, whose book *A Brush with Indian Art* won The Hindu Young World–Goodbooks Award 2019 for Best Book (Non-Fiction).

Charulata Mukherjee studies painting at the College of Art. She can be found sketching silly things all the time—in coffee shops, in the metro, at home—and her sketchbook is her biggest source of entertainment. She loves illustrating for children, especially because she believes that children can see in her illustrations what most adults can't.

About the Series

It's time to enter the fascinating
kingdom of insects with WWF India's
EEKS series! From bees to flies, from ants to
wasps and from mosquitoes to cockroaches, the
books in this unique series will introduce you to
a vast variety of insects we share our planet with
and help you discover some jaw-dropping facts
about them. So, what are you waiting for?
Bug out, have fun and be prepared
to be amazed!

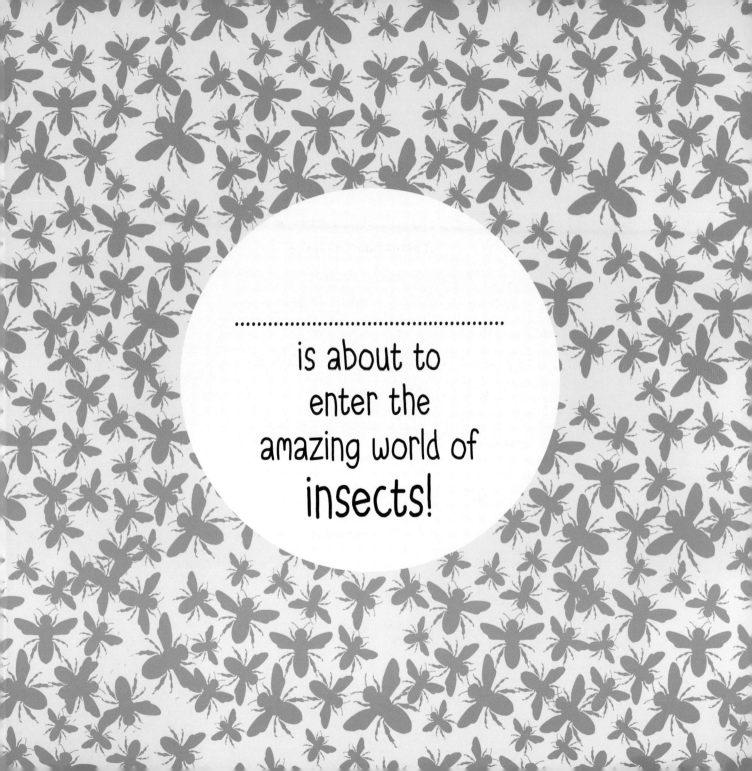

....

is about to
enter the
amazing world of
insects!

PUFFIN BOOKS

USA | Canada | UK | Ireland | Australia
New Zealand | India | South Africa | China

Puffin Books is part of the Penguin Random House group of companies
whose addresses can be found at global.penguinrandomhouse.com

Published by Penguin Random House India Pvt. Ltd
7th Floor, Infinity Tower C, DLF Cyber City,
Gurgaon 122 002, Haryana, India

First published in Puffin Books by Penguin Random House India 2021

Text and illustrations copyright © World Wide Fund for Nature-India 2021

ISBN 9780143451013

Layout and design by Aniruddha Mukherjee
Typeset in Bembo Infant by Syllables27, New Delhi
Printed at Aarvee Promotions, India

www.penguin.co.in

EEEEEEKKKS!

I SAW A BEE!

Arthy Muthanna Singh and Mamta Nainy

Illustrations by Charulata Mukherjee

WWF | 50 YEARS IN INDIA

PUFFIN BOOKS

An imprint of Penguin Random House

EEEEEEKKKS!

Did you see what just flew by,
Was it a bee, or was it a fly?
A bee it was, I'm telling you.
It looked busy and was buzzing too!

It's filling its hive with honey,
Golden, sweet and very yummy . . .
It might sting you, so keep away,
Don't touch its hive, keep it at bay!

What are the four words you think
of when you see a bee?

1. ....

2. ....

3. ....

4. ....

1

BOO!
Did you know that the fear of bees is called melissophobia (mel-iss-o-pho-bia) or apiphobia (api-pho-bia)?

2

BEES ARE BEAUTIFUL!

Have you ever watched a bee flitting from one colourful flower to another in a garden? Lovely sight, isn't it? Bees are flying insects related to wasps and ants. They are found on every continent except Antarctica. Some bees like to live alone while a great number of bee species live together in large groups called colonies. Each hive contains one colony.

There are nearly 20,000 known species of bees. They are categorized under different families or groups with really interesting names like carpenter bees, leafcutter bees, mason bees, honeybees, bumblebees and stingless bees. From Wallace's giant bee—which has a wingspan of 6 cm and a body size of an adult thumb—to the dwarf honeybee that is just 1.5 cm long and even smaller than a grain of rice, bees come in different sizes.

BEE-LIEVE IT!

The bee is an insect that has barely changed over millions of years. According to scientists, the earliest bee found was in Myanmar. It was found inside amber fossils, which have been dated to be 100 million years old. Amber is a tree resin, a sticky substance secreted by plants and trees to protect them from pests. And because it is meant to protect trees from pests, sometimes little organisms get stuck in the resin and remain there for millions of years, just like the bee did! Strange, isn't it?

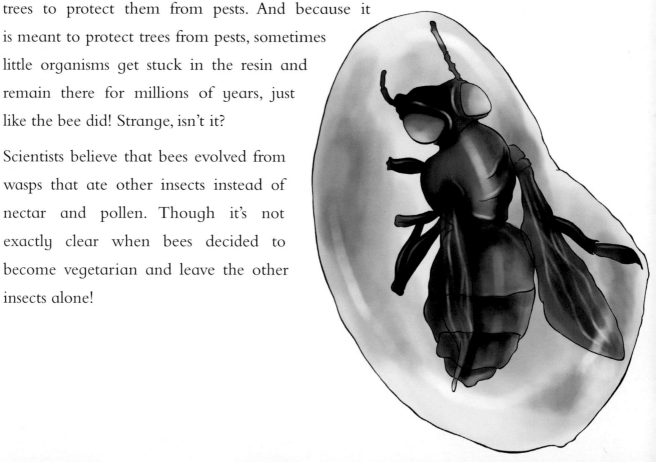

Scientists believe that bees evolved from wasps that ate other insects instead of nectar and pollen. Though it's not exactly clear when bees decided to become vegetarian and leave the other insects alone!

Bees have also been written about for hundreds of years. The ancient Romans believed that bees were messengers of the gods. If they saw a swarm of bees coming their way, they moved away because they believed they were carrying gods' messages.

The Greeks believed that if honey were placed on a baby's lips, it would be granted a gift of wisdom!

In ancient Egypt, it was believed that the sun god created the honeybee from his tears, and so, the ancient Egyptians regarded the bee as its royal symbol. In fact, Egyptians were the first ones to culture bees.

In Indian mythology too, bees have an important role. In India's oldest sacred book, the Rig Veda, you can read about bees and honey. Believe it or not, some people believe that the sting of the bee can ease the symptoms of certain diseases!

Like all insects, bees have six legs. Their bodies are divided into three parts: the head, thorax and abdomen. A bee has a furry body and face—especially bumblebees—which makes them look like flying teddy bears! A bee's head features two big compound eyes and three small simple ones. The head also has a pair of antennae that helps it to smell and the mandibles, the bee's jaws, which are used for almost everything—eating pollen, cutting and shaping wax, feeding larvae and the queen, cleaning the hive, grooming and fighting. The thorax of the bee is a body part between the head and the abdomen to which the wings and the legs are attached. A bee has two pairs of wings. Some species of bees like honeybees and bumblebees have a little basket on their hind legs to collect pollen.

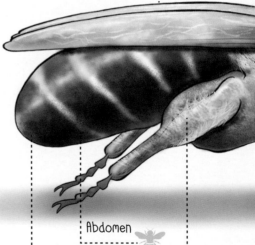

Two sets of transparent wings flap rapidly, more than 200 times per second

Feathered body hair help bees carry pollen. Bees have over three million hairs all over their bodies.

Abdomen

A stinger that's hidden until the bee is ready to sting

A pollen sac to store pollen

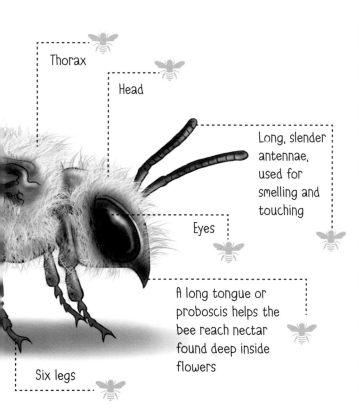

Thorax

Head

Long, slender antennae, used for smelling and touching

Eyes

A long tongue or proboscis helps the bee reach nectar found deep inside flowers

Six legs

PARTS OF A HONEYBEE

BET YOU DIDN'T KNOW THIS!

Inspired by the bee's anatomy, scientists at the Wyss Institute in the USA are developing RoboBees. Half the size of a paper clip, these tiny robots can fly and perch on plants. They can help in crop pollination, search and rescue operations as well as climate and environmental monitoring. Fascinating, isn't it?

Meet a ROBOTIC BEE!

EXOSKELETON

Bees, like all insects, have an exoskeleton—a hard exterior shell that protects what's inside their bodies. During cold days, bees are up very early in the morning. They vibrate their wing muscles in the thorax to generate heat, which enables them to stay active much before the sun is up.

IT'S A BEE'S LIFE!

Did you know that not all honeybees are the same type? There are three types or castes of bees in a colony: the queen, the female workers and the drones. While workers do the jobs that usually come to mind when we think of bees—finding food, building the honeycombs and protecting the hives—the queen and the drones have different functions. Let's find out about them and their very special jobs.

Queen bee

1. Just one per hive.
2. Largest bee in the colony. It has a curved stinger for defence.
3. Lays eggs and makes baby bees.
4. Releases chemical substances called pheromones to attract mates.
5. Lives for 2-3 years.

Drones

1. 300–500 per hive.
2. Smaller than the queen bee but bigger than the worker bees. They don't have a stinger.
3. Most drones do not live for more than ninety days. They usually die after mating with the queen.

Worker bees

1. 30,000–80,000 per hive.
2. Small females, which do not produce eggs. They have small stingers and die when they sting.
3. They find food; feed babies; build, protect and clean the hive; and make royal jelly to feed the queen.
4. Live for six weeks.

The queen can lay about 1000 to 1500 eggs every day, depending on the season, food availability and hive space. It may even lay a maximum of 6000 eggs per day!

A bee starts life as a tiny egg inside one of the many hexagonal cells made of wax in a special area of the hive. About 1 to 1.5 mm in size, the bee egg looks like a small grain of rice. A white grub called a larva hatches from the egg. Now the larva must eat and eat till it turns into a pupa. During the first 2–3 days, all larvae are fed on a special food called royal jelly, which is secreted by the glands of the young worker bees. It has water, proteins, sugars, vitamins and minerals. After that, they are given bee bread, which is a mixture of honey and pollen grain. The larvae that will become a queen in the future are fed only on royal jelly, and they are taken to the queen's special chamber. On the seventh day, the larva enters pupation. Now the worker bees cover the cell with a thin layer of wax. Inside the cell, the larva spins a cocoon around itself and turns into a pupa. During this time, the pupa develops recognizable features of a bee. Then the adult cuts the wall of the cocoon and chews its way out from the wax covering.

Life Cycle of a Bee

1. Egg
2. Larva
3. Pupa (Day 14)
4. Pupa (Day 18)
5. Adult

OF MANY KINDS

When we imagine a bee, the image that usually comes to mind is of a plump, fluffy black-and-yellow flying insect. But just like humans, bees also come in various shapes and sizes. Some are very big, while some are very small. Some are angry, some are peace-loving. Some can cook, some can build and some can dig—the sheer diversity in the bee world is breathtaking! Let's look at some of the most amazing bees in the bee kingdom.

KILLER BEES

Also known as Africanized honeybees, killer bees look like regular honeybees, but they sting ten times more and are fierce fighters. The story of how they came to be seems straight out of a sci-fi movie! In the year 1956, a scientist in Brazil named Warwick Kerr imported some honeybees from Africa to his laboratory. Some of the African honeybees escaped and mated with European honeybees, creating this fierce hybrid species. Killer bees can chase humans for over a quarter of a mile to defend their hives. They live in small colonies and are known to live in tires, crates, boxes and empty cars.

12 mm (*Apis mellifera scutellata*)

WALLACE'S GIANT BEE

Named after the British naturalist Alfred Wallace who first discovered this bee, Wallace's giant bee is a rare species found only in some Indonesian islands. With a wingspan of 2.5 inches, it's the world's largest bee. Lost for a good thirty-eight years, it was believed that this bee had gone extinct, but it made a dramatic comeback when a single female was rediscovered in the forests of Indonesia!

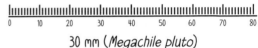
30 mm (*Megachile pluto*)

DWARF HONEYBEE

The dwarf honeybee is one of the world's smallest bees. The worker bees are less than 7–10 mm long—that's about twenty times smaller than the Wallace's giant bee. You might need a magnifying glass to see this one!

7–10 mm (*Apis florea*)

JAPANESE HONEYBEES

Would you believe us if we told you some bees can cook? Well, it's true! When giant hornets—a type of wasp—attack a colony of Japanese honeybees, the bees surround the intruder. They turn their body heat up to a temperature of 47°C and form a 'hot bee ball' around the enemy hornet, killing it within an hour.

75 mm (*Apis cerana japonica*)

A WORLD OF BEES!

Did we tell you there are over 20,000 different species of bees? The best known are social bees like honeybees and bumblebees who live in big families. But there are also many kinds of solitary bees in the bee world who live on their own. Some of these are leafcutter bees that cut pieces of leaves with their jaws to line their nests, European wool carder bees that strip hair from plants to weave their nests, carpenter bees that bore holes into wood to make their nests, cuckoo bees that lay eggs in the nests of other bees so their larvae can steal their food and lastly, hornfaced bees that do not have a queen and, instead, each female of this species lays eggs and makes her own nest cells of mud. There are also a lot of bees—around 500 species—whose stingers are so reduced that they are collectively referred to as stingless bees. Let's get to know some of them a little better.

HIMALAYAN HONEYBEES

Himalayan honeybees are social insects. As the name suggests, they live in one of the most challenging environments on Earth—the Himalayas. These are the world's largest honeybees and produce the world's most famous honey. They also build some of the most impressive cliff-edge nests.

30 mm (*Apis laboriosa*)

BLUE CARPENTER BEES

All bees are not yellow. Brilliant blue in colour, these carpenter bees lead solitary lives. They build nests just for themselves and only feed their own young; though sometimes several females might share the same nest. They get their name because they drill through wood to create their nests. They can be found throughout South East Asia, India and southern China.

23 mm (*Xylocopa caerulea*)

BUFF-TAILED BUMBLEBEES

Found throughout Europe, the buff-tailed bumblebees are large wild bees with dark yellow bands. They are named so because the queen bee has a buff-coloured tail—the colour of sand. Unlike honeybees, bumblebees can sting more than once because their stingers are smooth and do not get caught in the skin when they fly away after stinging.

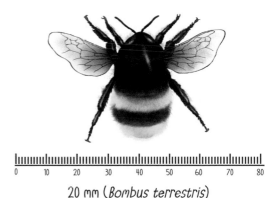

20 mm (*Bombus terrestris*)

ORCHARD MASON BEES

Also called the blue orchard bee, these bees are native to North America and Canada and are super pollinators. They are great at pollinating fruit crops and gardens and that's how they get their name. Using clay-like mud, they arrange their nests in partitions in reeds and natural holes.

20 mm (*Osmia lignaria propinqua Cresson*)

16

POLLEN POWER

When a bee sits on a flower, the flower's pollen rubs off on it, making it seem like the bee is covered with snow! When it travels to another flower, it brushes off the pollen on to it. This process of transferring pollen grains from the male part of a flower to the female is called pollination.

Without even realizing, bees are responsible for the pollination of food crops (vegetables, cereals, fruits), thereby providing a valuable service to humans free of charge. And what reward do the bees get for this fantastic pollination service? Yummy and healthy nectar, a sweet fluid found in flowers.

Plants adapt themselves according to their pollinators. Wind pollination is not very efficient. So, over thousands of years, flowers have been sporting bright colours and scents to attract bees.

Some plants such as in the family Solanaceae, which includes brinjal and tomatoes, are strictly bee-pollinated. When a bee visits, their pollen is loosened by the vibrations of the bee's wings, which is then collected by the bee as it visits one flower after the other, thereby pollinating them.

Many bees consume pollen, which is a rich source of protein. Because it's their main source of nutrition, you could think of it as their superfood. Bees store pollen, which later ferments into bee bread, in their hive next to the larvae. If they fail to do so, they may run short of food, especially in winter.

Bees also eat nectar, which they convert into honey and store in the cells of the honeycomb. Nectar is rich in carbohydrates. Sometimes, when there is less pollen and nectar, bees collect sweet juices from overripe fruits and honeydew secreted by insects and plant spores.

HONEY IS GOOD FOR YOU TOO!

A sample of honey is composed of water, sugar, minerals like calcium, iron, phosphate, manganese and about eight components of vitamin B complex. Honey is an antiseptic. One kilogram of honey contains 3200 calories. This energy-rich food is easy to digest, so it is fed to babies.

BEE HANG-OUTS!

Some bees spend their lives on their own, while some others live in large groups or colonies. A bee colony located in natural or artificial cavities is called a nest. It usually has a single entrance, facing downwards. Bees usually live in nests for several years. The inside of the nest has the honeycomb, an intriguing structure of hexagonal cells made of beeswax. All of it is made by bees without them even using a ruler! The bees use the cells to store food (honey and pollen) and to house the brood (eggs, larvae and pupae). A honeybee colony is often built in a tree hollow. But not all bees live in trees. Many of them also build their nests in caves, rock cavities or rotten wood. For instance, digger bees dig their nests in the ground, carpenter bees make their nests by hollowing the wood, mining bees make tunnels in the earth to make their nests, mason bees gather mud with which they build their nests and some bumblebees nest under a pile of leaves or stones or in abandoned mouse holes!

SHALL WE DANCE?

Did you know that bees dance? They sure do and are even fabulous at that! Worker bees find food and 'dance' to let other bees know about it. There are two main types of dances that they perform: round dance and waggle dance. Round dance is a movement in a circle. This is done to show that the food source is less than 50 m from the nest. The waggle dance is a figure-eight flight pattern. The bee waggles its abdomen to show that food is more than 150 m away. The exact distance can be shown by how long the dance lasts. A longer dance means a greater distance. Amazing, isn't it?

ROUND DANCE

WAGGLE DANCE

THE VANISHING BEES

Did you know that beekeepers and scientists all over the world are worried about bees because they are slowly vanishing? Yes, you read that right. Nobody seems to know the exact reason for their disappearance, but thousands and thousands of worker bees have been disappearing, leaving behind the queen, plenty of food and a few bees who take care of the baby bees and the queen. This mysterious condition is called the Colony Collapse Disorder. Scientists think it could be because of the loss of bees' habitats, infectious diseases, use of pesticides, global warming, etc., but they haven't been able to find the exact reason. The good news is that we can help . . . Here's how!

1. Plant flowers that provide nectar and pollen to bees.
2. Do not use chemical fertilizers or insecticides on the flowers.
3. Don't swat bees! You will be stopping the important work they do for the environment and for all of us.
4. If you find a beehive, leave it alone. Most bees don't sting, unless provoked.
5. Become a bee ambassador. Educate your friends and family on bees and get a buzz out of saving them!

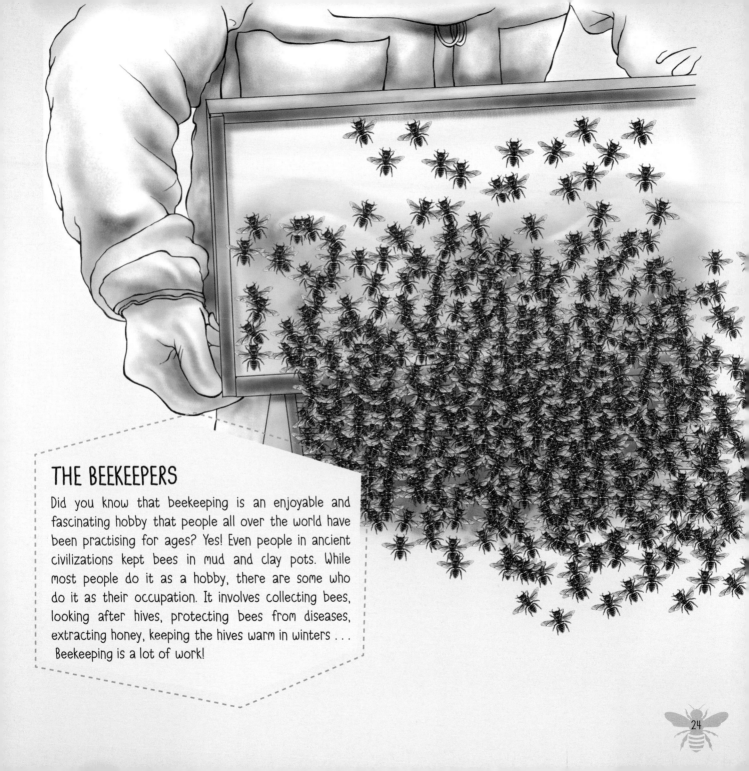

THE BEEKEEPERS

Did you know that beekeeping is an enjoyable and fascinating hobby that people all over the world have been practising for ages? Yes! Even people in ancient civilizations kept bees in mud and clay pots. While most people do it as a hobby, there are some who do it as their occupation. It involves collecting bees, looking after hives, protecting bees from diseases, extracting honey, keeping the hives warm in winters . . . Beekeeping is a lot of work!

24

WHAT BEES LIKE AND WHAT THEY DON'T

LIKE	DON'T LIKE
Sunshine	Pesticides
Nectar	Insects such as dragonflies, wax moths, wasps and arachnids
Pollen	Smoke
Flowers and fruit trees, apiaries	Honey badgers and bears
Honeycomb	Mothballs
Gardens, fields, forests	Bee-repelling plants such as mint, eucalyptus, citronella
Beekeepers	Humans who destroy their hives

THE BUZZING BEES

Now you know that bees are important members of our ecosystem. They don't just make honey, but a wide variety of bees also enable pollination for many plants, playing a huge role in their survival and the animals that need these plants to survive. Our survival, too, is heavily dependent on bees. These buzzing busybodies are truly a wonder of the insect kingdom!

YELLOW-FACED BEE

Found mostly in Hawaii, a yellow-faced bee is a small bee that is often mistaken for a wasp because of its colour. The yellow-faced bee is different from many other bees because it carries pollen in a special part of its stomach called the crop. These bees nest in tunnels or holes in wood and stems.

LAUGH OUT LOUD!

Why do bees hum?

Because they've forgotten the words!

BEES ARE COOL!

S o bees don't really deserve an EEKS, do they? Now, write four things that you think are amazing about bees.

1. ....

2. ....

3. ....

4. ....

WHAT'S THE BUZZ ABOUT?

You must have heard the buzz of the honeybee, but have you ever wondered why bees buzz? Buzzing is actually the sound of a bee's beating wings. For a bee to fly, its wings have to beat very fast. This is what produces the vibrations in the air that we hear as a buzzing sound!

SOME FUN WORDS TO KNOW ABOUT BEES

1. **Beehive:** A structure, made by beekeepers, in which some honeybees live. Have you ever seen a beehive?

2. **Honeycomb:** A sheet of six-sided cells made of beeswax.

3. **Ocelli:** The bee's simple eye.

4. **Pollen:** A fine powder containing pollen grains found on flowering plants.

5. **Nectar:** A sweet, sugary juice that flowers make.

Did you know?

1. The Nilgiri Biosphere Reserve—the first in India—is home to the giant honeybee, which forms honeycombs on steep cliff walls and in trees.

2. The bumblebee orchid mimics a female bee to ensure that male bees visit it for pollination.

3. Honeyguides are birds that only eat honey and actually led early humans to this superfood!

4. NASA conducted tests on bees on a shuttle, which showed that weightlessness did not affect bees and that they could reproduce as well as produce honeycombs.

5. Bees are great at maths! Some scientists have found out that bees can count up to four and can even add and subtract using very small numbers of nerve cells in their brains!

6. Dumbledore is the old English name for bumblebees—where else have you heard the name Dumbledore? (Hint: he's part of a pretty cool wizarding world!)

Activity 1

Apart from bees, which other insect makes you say EEKS?
Draw and colour it.

Activity 2

Think of a new species of bee and name it. Now draw it in the box below.
Try it; it'll be fun!

Be a critter spotter!

Our backyards are filled with small fascinating creatures. Go outside and explore the world of insects. Make notes of all the insects that you spot—their sizes, shapes and colours. To help with the exploration, carry a magnifying glass. Make sure you take time to observe. Take photos of the bugs you see or draw their pictures. Write down which bugs you see and where you saw them. From watching a centipede dig in the soil to seeing a bee interact with a flower, there is no limit to the number of things you can discover. But do remember that you're like a giant for a teeny bug—they might get scared of you! Watch them, but don't touch them or pick them up.

More reading on insects

https://kids.nationalgeographic.com/animals/invertebrates/insects/

https://www.si.edu/spotlight/buginfo/incredbugs

https://theconversation.com/birds-bees-and-bugs-your-garden-is-an-ecosystem-and-it-needs-looking-after-65226

https://www.coolkidfacts.com/insect-facts/

https://kids.britannica.com/

Insect Identification Sheet

Date: ....   Time: ....

Draw the insect	Habitat of the insect
	Describe where they are generally found in the world

1.   How many legs does the insect have?

2.   Does the insect have wings?

3.   Can you see its eyes?

4.   What colour is it?

5.   How many body parts does it have?

6.   Does it fly, hop or crawl?

Name of the insect: ....

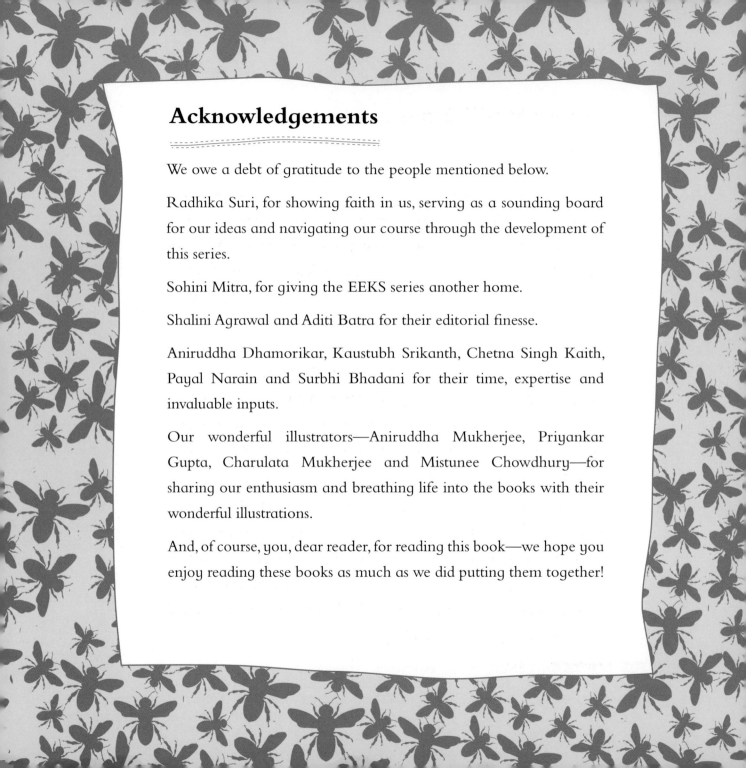

Acknowledgements

We owe a debt of gratitude to the people mentioned below.

Radhika Suri, for showing faith in us, serving as a sounding board for our ideas and navigating our course through the development of this series.

Sohini Mitra, for giving the EEKS series another home.

Shalini Agrawal and Aditi Batra for their editorial finesse.

Aniruddha Dhamorikar, Kaustubh Srikanth, Chetna Singh Kaith, Payal Narain and Surbhi Bhadani for their time, expertise and invaluable inputs.

Our wonderful illustrators—Aniruddha Mukherjee, Priyankar Gupta, Charulata Mukherjee and Mistunee Chowdhury—for sharing our enthusiasm and breathing life into the books with their wonderful illustrations.

And, of course, you, dear reader, for reading this book—we hope you enjoy reading these books as much as we did putting them together!

About WWF India

Marking fifty years of conservation in the country, WWF India works towards finding science-based and sustainable solutions to address challenges at the interface between development and conservation. Today, with over seventy offices across twenty states, WWF India's work spans thematic areas including the conservation of key wildlife species and their habitats; management of rivers, wetlands and their ecosystems; climate change adaptation; driving sustainable solutions for business and agriculture; empowering local communities; combatting illegal wildlife trade; and inspiring children and youth to take positive action for the environment through education and awareness programmes. WWF India is part of the WWF International Network, which has offices in more than 100 countries across the globe.

Environment Education has been a core part of WWF India since its inception in 1969. It continuously works to inform and empower the children, youth and citizens of India to act and create impact for a sustainable planet. Its initiatives reach out to diverse audiences and aim to create a generation of critical thinkers, problem-solvers and environmentally aware individuals.

Read More in the Series

  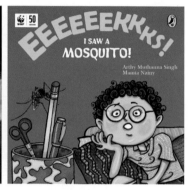

Ants are small but that's not all! Enter the jaw-dropping world of ants and explore some interesting facts about one of the most hard-working critters of the insect kingdom!

Whether cockroaches fill you with dread or wide-eyed wonder, there's no denying the fact that they are some of the most amazing creatures of the insect universe. So, dash right into their wonderful world, find out everything about them and be prepared to be super surprised!

Mosquitoes are mostly known as tiny troublemakers. But there are lots of interesting facts about these delicate insects. Read this book to find out about their many species, sizes, diets, homes and—most importantly—why they bite!